50 Sweets from Scratch to Bake

By: Kelly Johnson

Table of Contents

- Classic Chocolate Chip Cookies
- Soft Sugar Cookies
- Lemon Bars
- Carrot Cake
- Vanilla Cupcakes
- Brownies from Scratch
- Apple Pie with Homemade Crust
- Cinnamon Rolls
- Chocolate Fudge Cake
- Red Velvet Cake
- Homemade Shortbread Cookies
- Coconut Macaroons
- Blueberry Muffins
- Banana Bread
- Pumpkin Spice Bread
- Snickerdoodle Cookies
- Oatmeal Raisin Cookies

- Peach Cobbler
- Strawberry Rhubarb Pie
- Cherry Almond Scones
- Chocolate Chip Banana Bread
- Lemon Drizzle Cake
- Pecan Pie
- Coconut Cream Pie
- S'mores Bars
- Chocolate Tart with Ganache
- Key Lime Pie
- Molasses Cookies
- Chocolate Whoopie Pies
- Almond Joy Bars
- Chocolate Peanut Butter Cookies
- Cinnamon Sugar Palmiers
- Chocolate Brownie Bites
- Almond Biscotti
- Meringue Cookies
- Caramel Apple Cheesecake

- Pear and Almond Galette
- Pineapple Upside-Down Cake
- Raspberry Cream Cheese Danish
- Gingerbread Cookies
- Churros
- Buttermilk Biscuits with Jam
- Apple Cinnamon Muffins
- Salted Caramel Chocolate Cake
- Raspberry Almond Crumble Bars
- Maple Pecan Shortbread
- Lemon Meringue Bars
- Chocolate Covered Pretzels
- Poppy Seed Lemon Cake
- Toffee Almond Cookies

Classic Chocolate Chip Cookies

- **Ingredients**:

    1. 2 1/4 cups all-purpose flour
    2. 1/2 tsp baking soda
    3. 1 cup unsalted butter, softened
    4. 1/2 cup granulated sugar
    5. 1 cup packed brown sugar
    6. 2 tsp vanilla extract
    7. 2 large eggs
    8. 2 cups semi-sweet chocolate chips
    9. 1/2 tsp salt

- **Instructions**:

    1. Preheat oven to 350°F (175°C). Line a baking sheet with parchment paper.
    2. In a bowl, whisk together flour, baking soda, and salt.
    3. In a separate bowl, cream butter, granulated sugar, and brown sugar until smooth.
    4. Add eggs one at a time and vanilla extract, mixing until smooth.
    5. Gradually add the dry ingredients and fold in chocolate chips.
    6. Drop tablespoon-sized dough onto the baking sheet.
    7. Bake for 10–12 minutes until golden brown. Cool on wire racks.

Soft Sugar Cookies

- **Ingredients**:

    1. 2 3/4 cups all-purpose flour
    2. 1 tsp baking soda
    3. 1 tsp baking powder
    4. 1 1/2 cups unsalted butter, softened
    5. 1 1/2 cups granulated sugar
    6. 1 egg
    7. 1 tsp vanilla extract
    8. 1/2 tsp salt
    9. 1/4 cup granulated sugar (for rolling)

- **Instructions**:

    1. Preheat oven to 350°F (175°C). Line a baking sheet with parchment paper.
    2. In a bowl, whisk together flour, baking soda, baking powder, and salt.
    3. In a separate bowl, cream butter and 1 1/2 cups sugar.
    4. Add the egg and vanilla, mixing until smooth.
    5. Gradually add dry ingredients to the wet ingredients.
    6. Roll dough into balls and then roll them in the reserved sugar.
    7. Place on baking sheet and bake for 10-12 minutes. Let cool.

Lemon Bars

- **Ingredients**:

    1. **For the crust**:
        - 1 1/2 cups all-purpose flour
        - 1/2 cup powdered sugar
        - 1/2 cup unsalted butter, softened

    2. **For the filling**:
        - 2 large eggs
        - 1 1/2 cups granulated sugar
        - 1/4 cup all-purpose flour
        - 1/4 tsp baking powder
        - 1/4 cup fresh lemon juice
        - 1 tbsp lemon zest
        - Powdered sugar (for dusting)

- **Instructions**:

    1. Preheat oven to 350°F (175°C).
    2. For the crust, mix flour and powdered sugar. Cut in butter until crumbly. Press into a greased 9x9-inch pan.
    3. Bake for 15 minutes, then set aside to cool.

4. For the filling, whisk together eggs, sugar, flour, baking powder, lemon juice, and zest.

5. Pour over cooled crust and bake for 20–25 minutes.

6. Cool completely, then dust with powdered sugar.

Carrot Cake

- **Ingredients**:

    1. 2 cups all-purpose flour
    2. 2 tsp baking powder
    3. 1 tsp baking soda
    4. 1/2 tsp salt
    5. 1 1/2 tsp ground cinnamon
    6. 1 1/2 cups granulated sugar
    7. 1 cup vegetable oil
    8. 4 large eggs
    9. 2 cups grated carrots
    10. 1/2 cup crushed pineapple, drained
    11. 1/2 cup chopped walnuts (optional)
    12. **For the cream cheese frosting:**
        - 8 oz cream cheese, softened
        - 1/2 cup unsalted butter, softened
        - 4 cups powdered sugar
        - 1 tsp vanilla extract

- **Instructions**:

1. Preheat oven to 350°F (175°C). Grease and flour two 9-inch round cake pans.

2. In a bowl, whisk together flour, baking powder, baking soda, salt, and cinnamon.

3. In a separate bowl, mix sugar, oil, and eggs. Stir in grated carrots, pineapple, and walnuts.

4. Gradually fold in dry ingredients.

5. Pour batter into cake pans and bake for 30–35 minutes.

6. For frosting, beat cream cheese and butter until smooth. Gradually add powdered sugar and vanilla.

7. Frost cooled cakes and enjoy!

Vanilla Cupcakes

- **Ingredients**:

    1. 1 1/2 cups all-purpose flour
    2. 1 1/2 tsp baking powder
    3. 1/2 tsp salt
    4. 1/2 cup unsalted butter, softened
    5. 3/4 cup granulated sugar
    6. 2 large eggs
    7. 1 tsp vanilla extract
    8. 1/2 cup milk

- **Instructions**:

    1. Preheat oven to 350°F (175°C) and line a muffin tin with cupcake liners.
    2. In a bowl, whisk together flour, baking powder, and salt.
    3. In another bowl, cream butter and sugar. Add eggs one at a time, mixing well.
    4. Add vanilla extract and alternate adding dry ingredients and milk.
    5. Pour batter into cupcake liners, filling each 2/3 full.
    6. Bake for 18–20 minutes. Let cool.

Brownies from Scratch

- **Ingredients**:

    1. 1 cup unsalted butter
    2. 2 cups granulated sugar
    3. 1 cup unsweetened cocoa powder
    4. 1 tsp vanilla extract
    5. 4 large eggs
    6. 1 cup all-purpose flour
    7. 1/2 tsp salt
    8. 1/2 tsp baking powder

- **Instructions**:

    1. Preheat oven to 350°F (175°C). Grease a 9x13-inch pan.
    2. Melt butter and mix with sugar and cocoa powder.
    3. Stir in vanilla and eggs, one at a time.
    4. Fold in flour, salt, and baking powder.
    5. Pour into pan and bake for 30-35 minutes.

Apple Pie with Homemade Crust

- **Ingredients**:

    1. **For the crust**:
        - 2 1/2 cups all-purpose flour
        - 1 tbsp sugar
        - 1 tsp salt
        - 1 cup unsalted butter, cold and cubed
        - 6 tbsp ice water

    2. **For the filling**:
        - 6 cups peeled and sliced apples (Granny Smith or Honeycrisp)
        - 3/4 cup granulated sugar
        - 1/4 cup brown sugar
        - 1 1/2 tbsp cornstarch
        - 1/2 tsp ground cinnamon
        - 1/4 tsp ground nutmeg
        - 1 tbsp lemon juice

- **Instructions**:

    1. Preheat oven to 425°F (220°C).
    2. For the crust, combine flour, sugar, and salt. Cut in cold butter until the mixture resembles coarse crumbs. Add ice water and form a dough.

3. Roll dough into two discs. Place one in a pie pan and refrigerate.

4. For the filling, mix apples with sugar, brown sugar, cornstarch, cinnamon, nutmeg, and lemon juice.

5. Pour the filling into the pie crust, then cover with the second disc of dough. Cut slits in the top for steam to escape.

6. Bake for 45–50 minutes until golden brown. Cool before serving.

Cinnamon Rolls

- **Ingredients**:

    1. 4 cups all-purpose flour
    2. 1/4 cup sugar
    3. 2 1/4 tsp active dry yeast
    4. 1 cup warm milk
    5. 1/2 cup unsalted butter, melted
    6. 1 tsp salt
    7. 1/2 tsp ground cinnamon
    8. 1/2 cup brown sugar
    9. 2 tbsp butter, softened (for spreading)
    10. **For the icing**:
        - 1 cup powdered sugar
        - 2 tbsp milk
        - 1 tsp vanilla extract

- **Instructions**:

    1. In a bowl, combine flour, sugar, and yeast. Add warm milk, melted butter, salt, and cinnamon. Knead to form a dough.
    2. Let rise for 1–2 hours.

3. Roll out dough, spread softened butter, and sprinkle with brown sugar and cinnamon.

4. Roll up dough and cut into rolls. Place in a greased baking dish and let rise.

5. Preheat oven to 350°F (175°C) and bake for 20-25 minutes.

6. Mix powdered sugar, milk, and vanilla for icing. Drizzle over rolls.

Chocolate Fudge Cake

- **Ingredients**:

    1. 1 3/4 cups all-purpose flour
    2. 2 cups granulated sugar
    3. 1 cup unsweetened cocoa powder
    4. 1 tsp baking powder
    5. 1 1/2 tsp baking soda
    6. 1 tsp salt
    7. 2 large eggs
    8. 1 cup whole milk
    9. 1/2 cup vegetable oil
    10. 2 tsp vanilla extract
    11. 1 cup boiling water

- **Instructions**:

    1. Preheat oven to 350°F (175°C). Grease and flour two 9-inch round cake pans.
    2. In a large bowl, mix flour, sugar, cocoa powder, baking powder, baking soda, and salt.
    3. Add the eggs, milk, oil, and vanilla extract, mixing until smooth.
    4. Gradually add the boiling water to the batter, mixing until smooth. The batter will be thin.

5. Pour the batter into the prepared cake pans and bake for 30-35 minutes, or until a toothpick inserted into the center comes out clean.

6. Cool the cakes in the pans for 10 minutes, then remove from the pans and cool completely on a wire rack.

7. Frost with your favorite chocolate frosting, and enjoy!

Red Velvet Cake

- **Ingredients**:

    1. 2 1/2 cups all-purpose flour
    2. 1 1/2 cups granulated sugar
    3. 1 tsp baking powder
    4. 1 tsp baking soda
    5. 1 tsp salt
    6. 1 tbsp cocoa powder
    7. 1 1/2 cups vegetable oil
    8. 2 large eggs
    9. 1 cup buttermilk
    10. 2 tbsp red food coloring
    11. 1 tsp vanilla extract
    12. 1 tsp white vinegar

- **For the Cream Cheese Frosting**:

    1. 8 oz cream cheese, softened
    2. 1/2 cup unsalted butter, softened
    3. 4 cups powdered sugar
    4. 1 tsp vanilla extract

- **Instructions**:

    1. Preheat oven to 350°F (175°C). Grease and flour two 9-inch round cake pans.

    2. In a bowl, whisk together the flour, sugar, baking powder, baking soda, salt, and cocoa powder.

    3. In a separate bowl, beat the oil and eggs until smooth, then add the buttermilk, red food coloring, vanilla extract, and vinegar. Mix well.

    4. Gradually add the dry ingredients to the wet ingredients, mixing until combined.

    5. Pour the batter evenly into the cake pans and bake for 30-35 minutes, or until a toothpick inserted into the center comes out clean.

    6. Let the cakes cool in the pans for 10 minutes, then turn out onto a wire rack to cool completely.

    7. For the frosting, beat together the cream cheese, butter, powdered sugar, and vanilla until smooth and creamy.

    8. Frost the cooled cakes with the cream cheese frosting and enjoy!

Homemade Shortbread Cookies

- **Ingredients**:

    1. 2 cups all-purpose flour
    2. 1/2 cup granulated sugar
    3. 1 cup unsalted butter, softened
    4. 1/4 tsp salt
    5. 1 tsp vanilla extract

- **Instructions**:

    1. Preheat oven to 325°F (165°C). Line a baking sheet with parchment paper.
    2. In a large bowl, cream the butter and sugar until light and fluffy.
    3. Gradually add the flour and salt, mixing until combined. Add vanilla extract.
    4. Turn the dough out onto a lightly floured surface and roll it to about 1/4-inch thickness.
    5. Cut the dough into desired shapes using cookie cutters or a knife.
    6. Place the cookies onto the prepared baking sheet and bake for 12-15 minutes, or until the edges are golden brown.
    7. Cool the cookies on a wire rack. Optionally, you can sprinkle them with sugar or dip them in melted chocolate.

Coconut Macaroons

- Ingredients:

    1. 2 1/2 cups shredded coconut
    2. 2/3 cup sugar
    3. 1/4 cup all-purpose flour
    4. 1/4 tsp salt
    5. 4 large egg whites
    6. 1 tsp vanilla extract

- Instructions:

    1. Preheat oven to 325°F (163°C) and line a baking sheet with parchment paper.
    2. Mix shredded coconut, sugar, flour, and salt in a bowl.
    3. In a separate bowl, beat egg whites until stiff peaks form, then fold in the coconut mixture and vanilla extract.
    4. Drop spoonfuls of the mixture onto the baking sheet.
    5. Bake for 15–20 minutes or until golden brown.
    6. Let cool before serving.

Blueberry Muffins

- Ingredients:

    1. 2 cups all-purpose flour
    2. 1/2 cup sugar
    3. 1 tsp baking powder
    4. 1/2 tsp baking soda
    5. 1/4 tsp salt
    6. 1/2 cup milk
    7. 1/4 cup butter, melted
    8. 1 large egg
    9. 1 1/2 cups fresh blueberries

- Instructions:

    1. Preheat oven to 375°F (190°C) and line a muffin tin with paper liners.
    2. Mix dry ingredients (flour, sugar, baking powder, baking soda, and salt) in a bowl.
    3. In another bowl, whisk together milk, melted butter, and egg.
    4. Fold the wet ingredients into the dry ingredients until combined.
    5. Gently fold in the blueberries.
    6. Spoon the batter into muffin cups and bake for 20–25 minutes or until golden.

7. Let cool before serving.

Banana Bread

- Ingredients:

    1. 2 to 3 ripe bananas, mashed
    2. 1/2 cup butter, softened
    3. 3/4 cup sugar
    4. 2 large eggs
    5. 1 1/2 cups all-purpose flour
    6. 1 tsp baking soda
    7. 1/4 tsp salt
    8. 1 tsp vanilla extract

- Instructions:

    1. Preheat oven to 350°F (175°C) and grease a loaf pan.
    2. In a large bowl, cream together butter and sugar, then add eggs and mashed bananas.
    3. Stir in flour, baking soda, salt, and vanilla.
    4. Pour the batter into the loaf pan and bake for 60–65 minutes.
    5. Cool for 10 minutes before removing from the pan.

Pumpkin Spice Bread

- Ingredients:

    1. 1 3/4 cups all-purpose flour
    2. 1 tsp baking soda
    3. 1/2 tsp baking powder
    4. 1 1/2 tsp cinnamon
    5. 1/2 tsp ground nutmeg
    6. 1/4 tsp ground ginger
    7. 1/4 tsp salt
    8. 1 cup pumpkin puree
    9. 1 cup sugar
    10. 1/2 cup vegetable oil
    11. 2 large eggs
    12. 1 tsp vanilla extract

- Instructions:

    1. Preheat oven to 350°F (175°C) and grease a loaf pan.
    2. Mix dry ingredients (flour, baking soda, baking powder, cinnamon, nutmeg, ginger, and salt).
    3. In another bowl, combine pumpkin puree, sugar, oil, eggs, and vanilla.
    4. Stir wet ingredients into the dry ingredients.

5. Pour batter into the loaf pan and bake for 60–65 minutes or until a toothpick comes out clean.

6. Let cool before serving.

Snickerdoodle Cookies

- Ingredients:

    1. 2 3/4 cups all-purpose flour
    2. 1 tsp baking soda
    3. 1/2 tsp cream of tartar
    4. 1/2 tsp salt
    5. 1 cup unsalted butter, softened
    6. 1 1/2 cups sugar
    7. 2 large eggs
    8. 2 tbsp sugar (for rolling)
    9. 2 tsp ground cinnamon (for rolling)

- Instructions:

    1. Preheat oven to 350°F (175°C).
    2. In a bowl, whisk together flour, baking soda, cream of tartar, and salt.
    3. Cream together butter and sugar, then add eggs and mix well.
    4. Gradually add the dry ingredients to the wet ingredients, mixing until combined.
    5. In a small bowl, mix sugar and cinnamon.
    6. Roll dough into balls, then coat in the cinnamon-sugar mixture.
    7. Place on a baking sheet and bake for 10–12 minutes.

8. Let cool on a wire rack before serving.

Oatmeal Raisin Cookies

- Ingredients:

    1. 1 1/2 cups all-purpose flour
    2. 1 tsp baking soda
    3. 1/2 tsp cinnamon
    4. 1/4 tsp salt
    5. 1 cup unsalted butter, softened
    6. 1 cup brown sugar, packed
    7. 2 large eggs
    8. 1 1/2 cups rolled oats
    9. 1 cup raisins

- Instructions:

    1. Preheat oven to 350°F (175°C).
    2. In a bowl, whisk together flour, baking soda, cinnamon, and salt.
    3. Cream together butter and brown sugar, then add eggs and mix well.
    4. Gradually add dry ingredients to wet ingredients, then stir in oats and raisins.
    5. Drop spoonfuls of dough onto a baking sheet.
    6. Bake for 10–12 minutes or until golden.
    7. Cool on a wire rack.

Peach Cobbler

- Ingredients:

    1. 4 cups fresh or frozen peaches, sliced
    2. 1/2 cup sugar
    3. 1 tbsp cornstarch
    4. 1/4 tsp cinnamon
    5. 1 tbsp lemon juice
    6. 1 1/2 cups all-purpose flour
    7. 2 tbsp sugar
    8. 1/2 tsp salt
    9. 1/2 tsp baking powder
    10. 1/2 cup milk
    11. 1/4 cup unsalted butter, melted

- Instructions:

    1. Preheat oven to 375°F (190°C).
    2. In a bowl, mix peaches with sugar, cornstarch, cinnamon, and lemon juice.
    3. Pour the peach mixture into a baking dish.
    4. In another bowl, mix flour, sugar, salt, and baking powder.
    5. Stir in milk and melted butter until a thick batter forms.

6. Spoon batter over peaches and bake for 40–45 minutes.

7. Let cool slightly before serving.

Strawberry Rhubarb Pie

- Ingredients:

    1. 2 cups fresh rhubarb, chopped
    2. 2 cups fresh strawberries, hulled and halved
    3. 1 1/4 cups sugar
    4. 1/4 cup cornstarch
    5. 1/4 tsp salt
    6. 1 tbsp lemon juice
    7. 1 package pie crust (or homemade)

- Instructions:

    1. Preheat oven to 425°F (220°C).
    2. In a bowl, mix rhubarb, strawberries, sugar, cornstarch, salt, and lemon juice.
    3. Line a pie dish with the bottom pie crust.
    4. Pour the fruit mixture into the crust.
    5. Cover with the top pie crust, seal edges, and cut slits to vent.
    6. Bake for 45–50 minutes, or until the crust is golden.
    7. Cool before serving.

Cherry Almond Scones

- Ingredients:
    1. 2 cups all-purpose flour
    2. 1/2 cup sugar
    3. 2 1/2 tsp baking powder
    4. 1/4 tsp salt
    5. 1/2 cup cold unsalted butter, cubed
    6. 1/2 cup buttermilk
    7. 1/2 tsp almond extract
    8. 1 cup cherries, pitted and chopped
    9. 1/4 cup sliced almonds
- Instructions:
    1. Preheat oven to 375°F (190°C) and line a baking sheet with parchment paper.
    2. In a bowl, whisk together flour, sugar, baking powder, and salt.
    3. Cut in the butter until the mixture resembles coarse crumbs.
    4. Stir in buttermilk, almond extract, cherries, and sliced almonds.
    5. Turn the dough onto a floured surface, pat it into a circle, and cut into wedges.
    6. Bake for 20–25 minutes until golden.

7. Cool before serving.

Chocolate Chip Banana Bread

- Ingredients:

    1. 2 to 3 ripe bananas, mashed
    2. 1/2 cup unsalted butter, softened
    3. 3/4 cup sugar
    4. 2 large eggs
    5. 1 1/2 cups all-purpose flour
    6. 1/2 tsp baking soda
    7. 1/4 tsp salt
    8. 1 cup chocolate chips

- Instructions:

    1. Preheat oven to 350°F (175°C) and grease a loaf pan.
    2. Cream together butter and sugar, then add eggs and mashed bananas.
    3. Stir in flour, baking soda, and salt.
    4. Fold in chocolate chips.
    5. Pour batter into the loaf pan and bake for 60–65 minutes.
    6. Cool before serving.

Lemon Drizzle Cake

- Ingredients:

    1. 1 1/2 cups all-purpose flour
    2. 1 1/2 tsp baking powder
    3. 1/4 tsp salt
    4. 1/2 cup unsalted butter, softened
    5. 1 cup sugar
    6. 2 large eggs
    7. 1/2 cup milk
    8. Zest of 1 lemon
    9. 1/4 cup lemon juice
    10. 1/2 cup powdered sugar (for glaze)

- Instructions:

    1. Preheat oven to 350°F (175°C) and grease a loaf pan.
    2. Whisk together flour, baking powder, and salt.
    3. Cream together butter and sugar, then add eggs and beat well.
    4. Stir in milk, lemon zest, and lemon juice.
    5. Add dry ingredients and mix until combined.
    6. Bake for 40–45 minutes.

7. For the glaze, mix powdered sugar with lemon juice and drizzle over the cake.

8. Let cool before serving.

Pecan Pie

- Ingredients:

    1. 1 pie crust (store-bought or homemade)
    2. 1 cup corn syrup
    3. 1 cup sugar
    4. 1/4 cup unsalted butter, melted
    5. 3 large eggs
    6. 1 1/2 cups pecans
    7. 1 tsp vanilla extract

- Instructions:

    1. Preheat oven to 350°F (175°C).
    2. In a bowl, whisk together corn syrup, sugar, butter, eggs, and vanilla extract.
    3. Stir in pecans.
    4. Pour the mixture into the prepared pie crust.
    5. Bake for 50–55 minutes, or until the filling is set.
    6. Cool before serving.

Coconut Cream Pie

- Ingredients:

    1. 1 pie crust, baked
    2. 1 1/2 cups whole milk
    3. 1/2 cup sugar
    4. 1/4 cup cornstarch
    5. 1/4 tsp salt
    6. 3 large egg yolks
    7. 1 cup shredded coconut
    8. 1 tsp vanilla extract
    9. 1 cup heavy cream
    10. 2 tbsp sugar (for whipped cream)

- Instructions:

    1. In a saucepan, whisk together milk, sugar, cornstarch, and salt over medium heat.
    2. In a separate bowl, whisk egg yolks. Gradually add some hot milk mixture to the yolks, then return to the saucepan and cook until thickened.
    3. Stir in coconut and vanilla extract.
    4. Pour the mixture into the baked pie crust and refrigerate until set.
    5. Whip the cream with sugar and top the pie.

6. Serve chilled.

S'mores Bars

- Ingredients:

    1. 1 1/2 cups graham cracker crumbs
    2. 1/2 cup sugar
    3. 1/2 cup butter, melted
    4. 2 cups chocolate chips
    5. 1 1/2 cups mini marshmallows

- Instructions:

    1. Preheat oven to 350°F (175°C) and grease a baking pan.
    2. Mix graham cracker crumbs, sugar, and butter.
    3. Press the mixture into the bottom of the pan.
    4. Bake for 10–12 minutes, then remove from the oven.
    5. Sprinkle chocolate chips and marshmallows over the crust.
    6. Bake for an additional 5–7 minutes.
    7. Cool and cut into bars.

Chocolate Tart with Ganache

- Ingredients:

    1. 1 tart crust (store-bought or homemade)
    2. 8 oz dark chocolate
    3. 1 cup heavy cream
    4. 1 tbsp sugar
    5. 1 tsp vanilla extract

- Instructions:

    1. Preheat oven to 350°F (175°C) and bake the tart crust for 10 minutes.
    2. In a saucepan, heat the cream and sugar until simmering.
    3. Pour over the chocolate and stir until smooth.
    4. Add vanilla extract and pour into the tart crust.
    5. Refrigerate for 2 hours or until set.
    6. Serve chilled.

Key Lime Pie

- Ingredients:

    1. 1 graham cracker crust
    2. 1 can sweetened condensed milk
    3. 1/2 cup key lime juice
    4. 3 large egg yolks
    5. 1 cup heavy cream
    6. 2 tbsp sugar (for whipped cream)

- Instructions:

    1. Preheat oven to 350°F (175°C).
    2. In a bowl, whisk together condensed milk, key lime juice, and egg yolks.
    3. Pour into the graham cracker crust and bake for 10 minutes.
    4. Chill for at least 3 hours.
    5. Whip the cream with sugar and top the pie before serving.

Molasses Cookies

- Ingredients:

    1. 2 1/4 cups all-purpose flour
    2. 1 tsp baking soda
    3. 1/2 tsp cinnamon
    4. 1/2 tsp ground ginger
    5. 1/4 tsp ground cloves
    6. 1/4 tsp salt
    7. 3/4 cup unsalted butter, softened
    8. 1 cup sugar
    9. 1/4 cup molasses
    10. 1 large egg
    11. 1/4 cup sugar (for rolling)

- Instructions:

    1. Preheat oven to 350°F (175°C) and line a baking sheet with parchment paper.
    2. In a bowl, whisk together flour, baking soda, cinnamon, ginger, cloves, and salt.
    3. Cream together butter and sugar, then add molasses and egg.
    4. Gradually add the dry ingredients and mix until combined.

5. Roll dough into balls and coat with sugar.

6. Place on the baking sheet and bake for 10–12 minutes.

7. Cool before serving.

Chocolate Whoopie Pies

- Ingredients:

    1. 2 1/2 cups all-purpose flour
    2. 1 1/2 tsp baking powder
    3. 1 tsp cocoa powder
    4. 1/2 tsp baking soda
    5. 1/4 tsp salt
    6. 1/2 cup unsalted butter, softened
    7. 1 cup sugar
    8. 2 large eggs
    9. 1 cup buttermilk
    10. 1 tsp vanilla extract
    11. 1/2 cup cocoa powder (for filling)
    12. 1/2 cup powdered sugar (for filling)
    13. 1/4 cup butter, softened (for filling)
    14. 1 tsp vanilla extract (for filling)
    15. 1 1/2 cups marshmallow fluff (for filling)

- Instructions:

    1. Preheat oven to 350°F (175°C) and line a baking sheet with parchment paper.

2. In a bowl, whisk together flour, baking powder, cocoa powder, baking soda, and salt.

3. Cream together butter and sugar, then add eggs and mix.

4. Gradually add dry ingredients, alternating with buttermilk, and mix in vanilla.

5. Drop spoonfuls of dough onto the baking sheet and bake for 10–12 minutes.

6. Cool completely.

7. For the filling, mix together cocoa powder, powdered sugar, butter, vanilla, and marshmallow fluff.

8. Spread the filling between two cookies to form sandwiches.

Almond Joy Bars

- Ingredients:

    1. 1 1/2 cups shredded coconut
    2. 1/2 cup powdered sugar
    3. 2 tbsp milk
    4. 1/2 tsp vanilla extract
    5. 1 cup almonds
    6. 1 cup semisweet chocolate chips
    7. 1 tbsp coconut oil

- Instructions:

    1. Line a baking pan with parchment paper.
    2. In a bowl, mix coconut, powdered sugar, milk, and vanilla extract until combined.
    3. Press the coconut mixture into the baking pan.
    4. Top with almonds.
    5. In a microwave-safe bowl, melt chocolate chips and coconut oil together until smooth.
    6. Pour the chocolate mixture over the coconut and almonds.
    7. Refrigerate until set, about 2 hours.
    8. Cut into bars.

Chocolate Peanut Butter Cookies

- Ingredients:

    1. 1 cup peanut butter
    2. 1 cup sugar
    3. 1 large egg
    4. 1 tsp vanilla extract
    5. 1/4 cup cocoa powder
    6. 1/4 tsp baking soda
    7. 1/4 tsp salt

- Instructions:

    1. Preheat oven to 350°F (175°C) and line a baking sheet with parchment paper.
    2. Mix together peanut butter, sugar, egg, and vanilla extract.
    3. Stir in cocoa powder, baking soda, and salt.
    4. Drop spoonfuls of dough onto the baking sheet.
    5. Press down with a fork in a criss-cross pattern.
    6. Bake for 8–10 minutes.
    7. Cool before serving.

Cinnamon Sugar Palmiers

- Ingredients:

    1. 1 sheet puff pastry, thawed
    2. 1/2 cup sugar
    3. 1 tbsp ground cinnamon
    4. 1/4 cup melted butter

- Instructions:

    1. Preheat oven to 400°F (200°C) and line a baking sheet with parchment paper.
    2. Roll out the puff pastry sheet and brush with melted butter.
    3. Mix sugar and cinnamon, then sprinkle evenly over the pastry.
    4. Fold the edges of the pastry towards the center, then fold in half.
    5. Slice the dough into 1/2-inch pieces and place on the baking sheet.
    6. Bake for 10–12 minutes or until golden.
    7. Let cool before serving.

Chocolate Brownie Bites

- Ingredients:

    1. 1/2 cup unsalted butter, melted
    2. 1 cup sugar
    3. 1/2 cup cocoa powder
    4. 2 large eggs
    5. 1 tsp vanilla extract
    6. 1/2 cup all-purpose flour
    7. 1/4 tsp salt
    8. 1/4 tsp baking powder

- Instructions:

    1. Preheat oven to 350°F (175°C) and grease a mini muffin tin.
    2. In a bowl, mix together melted butter, sugar, cocoa powder, eggs, and vanilla.
    3. Stir in flour, salt, and baking powder.
    4. Spoon the batter into the muffin tin and bake for 10–12 minutes.
    5. Cool before serving.

Almond Biscotti

- Ingredients:
    1. 1 1/2 cups all-purpose flour
    2. 1 cup sugar
    3. 1 tsp baking powder
    4. 1/2 tsp salt
    5. 2 large eggs
    6. 1 tsp vanilla extract
    7. 1/2 cup whole almonds
- Instructions:
    1. Preheat oven to 350°F (175°C) and line a baking sheet with parchment paper.
    2. Mix together flour, sugar, baking powder, and salt.
    3. Add eggs and vanilla extract, and stir until a dough forms.
    4. Stir in almonds.
    5. Shape dough into a log and bake for 25 minutes.
    6. Remove from the oven, cool slightly, then slice into 1/2-inch pieces.
    7. Bake slices for an additional 10–15 minutes until crisp.

Meringue Cookies

- Ingredients:

    1. 4 large egg whites
    2. 1 cup sugar
    3. 1/4 tsp vanilla extract
    4. Pinch of salt

- Instructions:

    1. Preheat oven to 200°F (93°C) and line a baking sheet with parchment paper.
    2. In a bowl, beat egg whites until soft peaks form.
    3. Gradually add sugar, a tablespoon at a time, and continue beating until stiff peaks form.
    4. Add vanilla and salt.
    5. Spoon or pipe the meringue onto the baking sheet.
    6. Bake for 1–1.5 hours until crisp.
    7. Cool completely before serving.

Caramel Apple Cheesecake

- Ingredients:

    1. 1 premade graham cracker crust
    2. 3 cups cream cheese, softened
    3. 1 cup sugar
    4. 2 large eggs
    5. 1 tsp vanilla extract
    6. 1 1/2 cups apples, peeled and chopped
    7. 1/2 cup caramel sauce

- Instructions:

    1. Preheat oven to 325°F (160°C).
    2. Beat cream cheese and sugar until smooth, then add eggs one at a time and mix in vanilla.
    3. Pour the mixture into the graham cracker crust and bake for 45–50 minutes.
    4. Let cool.
    5. Top with chopped apples and drizzle with caramel sauce before serving.

Pear and Almond Galette

- Ingredients:

    1. 1 sheet puff pastry
    2. 2 ripe pears, sliced
    3. 1/2 cup almond meal
    4. 1/4 cup sugar
    5. 1 tbsp butter, cut into small pieces

- Instructions:

    1. Preheat oven to 375°F (190°C) and line a baking sheet with parchment paper.
    2. Roll out puff pastry and sprinkle with almond meal.
    3. Arrange pear slices in the center and fold the edges of the pastry over.
    4. Sprinkle with sugar and dot with butter.
    5. Bake for 25–30 minutes or until golden brown.
    6. Cool before serving.

Pineapple Upside-Down Cake

- Ingredients:

    1. 1/2 cup butter
    2. 1 cup brown sugar
    3. 1 can pineapple rings
    4. 1 jar maraschino cherries
    5. 1 1/2 cups all-purpose flour
    6. 1 cup sugar
    7. 1/2 tsp baking powder
    8. 1/2 tsp baking soda
    9. 1/4 tsp salt
    10. 1/2 cup milk
    11. 2 large eggs

- Instructions:

    1. Preheat oven to 350°F (175°C).
    2. Melt butter in a pan and stir in brown sugar.
    3. Arrange pineapple rings and cherries in the bottom of the pan.
    4. In a separate bowl, mix flour, sugar, baking powder, baking soda, salt, milk, and eggs.
    5. Pour batter over the pineapple and bake for 40–45 minutes.

6. Let cool, then invert the cake to serve.

Raspberry Cream Cheese Danish

- Ingredients:

    1. 1 sheet puff pastry
    2. 8 oz cream cheese, softened
    3. 1/4 cup sugar
    4. 1 tsp vanilla extract
    5. 1/2 cup fresh raspberries
    6. 1 egg (for egg wash)

- Instructions:

    1. Preheat oven to 375°F (190°C) and line a baking sheet with parchment paper.
    2. Roll out puff pastry and cut into squares.
    3. Mix cream cheese, sugar, and vanilla.
    4. Spoon cream cheese mixture into the center of each square, top with raspberries, and fold edges.
    5. Brush with egg wash and bake for 15–20 minutes or until golden.
    6. Cool before serving.

Gingerbread Cookies

- Ingredients:

    1. 3 1/4 cups all-purpose flour
    2. 1 tsp baking soda
    3. 2 tbsp ground ginger
    4. 1 tbsp ground cinnamon
    5. 1/2 tsp ground cloves
    6. 1/2 tsp ground nutmeg
    7. 1/2 tsp salt
    8. 3/4 cup unsalted butter, softened
    9. 1 cup brown sugar, packed
    10. 1 large egg
    11. 1/2 cup molasses
    12. 1 tsp vanilla extract

- Instructions:

    1. Preheat oven to 350°F (175°C).
    2. In a bowl, whisk together flour, baking soda, spices, and salt.
    3. Cream butter and brown sugar until light and fluffy.
    4. Add egg, molasses, and vanilla, and mix until combined.

5. Gradually add the dry ingredients and mix until a dough forms.

6. Roll dough into 1/4-inch thick sheets, cut into shapes, and place on a baking sheet.

7. Bake for 8–10 minutes. Cool before decorating.

Churros

- Ingredients:
    1. 1 cup water
    2. 1/2 cup unsalted butter
    3. 1 1/4 cups all-purpose flour
    4. 1/4 tsp salt
    5. 1 tbsp sugar
    6. 3 large eggs
    7. Vegetable oil (for frying)
    8. 1/2 cup sugar (for coating)
    9. 1 tsp cinnamon (for coating)
- Instructions:
    1. In a saucepan, bring water and butter to a boil.
    2. Stir in flour, salt, and sugar, and cook for 2-3 minutes until the dough pulls away from the sides.
    3. Remove from heat, then mix in eggs one at a time until smooth.
    4. Heat oil in a deep pan for frying.
    5. Pipe dough into 4-inch strips and fry until golden.
    6. Drain on paper towels, then roll in cinnamon sugar.

Buttermilk Biscuits with Jam

- Ingredients:

    1. 2 cups all-purpose flour
    2. 1 tbsp baking powder
    3. 1/2 tsp salt
    4. 1/2 cup unsalted butter, cold
    5. 3/4 cup buttermilk

- Instructions:

    1. Preheat oven to 450°F (230°C).
    2. In a bowl, combine flour, baking powder, and salt.
    3. Cut in cold butter until the mixture resembles coarse crumbs.
    4. Stir in buttermilk until a dough forms.
    5. Turn dough onto a floured surface and knead 3-4 times.
    6. Roll out to 1-inch thick and cut with a biscuit cutter.
    7. Place on a baking sheet and bake for 10-12 minutes.
    8. Serve warm with jam.

Apple Cinnamon Muffins

- Ingredients:

    1. 2 cups all-purpose flour
    2. 1 tsp baking soda
    3. 1 tsp ground cinnamon
    4. 1/4 tsp salt
    5. 1/2 cup unsalted butter, softened
    6. 1 cup sugar
    7. 2 large eggs
    8. 1 cup applesauce
    9. 1 tsp vanilla extract
    10. 1/2 cup diced apples

- Instructions:

    1. Preheat oven to 350°F (175°C) and line a muffin tin with paper liners.
    2. In a bowl, whisk together flour, baking soda, cinnamon, and salt.
    3. Cream butter and sugar, then add eggs one at a time.
    4. Stir in applesauce and vanilla, then fold in the dry ingredients.
    5. Add diced apples and mix.
    6. Spoon batter into muffin cups and bake for 20-25 minutes.

Salted Caramel Chocolate Cake

- Ingredients:

    1. 1 1/2 cups all-purpose flour
    2. 1 tsp baking powder
    3. 1/2 tsp baking soda
    4. 1/4 tsp salt
    5. 1/2 cup unsalted butter, softened
    6. 1 cup sugar
    7. 2 large eggs
    8. 1 tsp vanilla extract
    9. 1/2 cup cocoa powder
    10. 1 cup buttermilk
    11. 1 cup heavy cream (for caramel)
    12. 1/2 cup brown sugar (for caramel)
    13. 1/4 tsp sea salt (for topping)

- Instructions:

    1. Preheat oven to 350°F (175°C) and grease two 9-inch cake pans.
    2. In a bowl, whisk together flour, baking powder, baking soda, salt, and cocoa powder.
    3. In another bowl, cream butter and sugar. Add eggs and vanilla.

4. Alternate adding the dry ingredients and buttermilk until smooth.

5. Pour batter into prepared pans and bake for 25-30 minutes.

6. For the caramel, heat heavy cream and brown sugar in a saucepan until simmering.

7. Pour over cake layers, and sprinkle with sea salt.

Raspberry Almond Crumble Bars

- Ingredients:

    1. 1 1/2 cups all-purpose flour
    2. 1/2 cup sugar
    3. 1/2 cup butter, softened
    4. 1/4 tsp almond extract
    5. 1/2 cup raspberry jam
    6. 1/4 cup sliced almonds

- Instructions:

    1. Preheat oven to 350°F (175°C) and grease a baking dish.
    2. In a bowl, combine flour, sugar, and butter. Mix until crumbly.
    3. Press 2/3 of the dough into the bottom of the dish.
    4. Spread raspberry jam over the dough.
    5. Crumble the remaining dough on top and sprinkle with almonds.
    6. Bake for 30-35 minutes until golden.

Maple Pecan Shortbread

- Ingredients:

    1. 2 cups all-purpose flour
    2. 1/2 cup cornstarch
    3. 1/2 tsp salt
    4. 1 cup unsalted butter, softened
    5. 1/2 cup powdered sugar
    6. 1/4 cup maple syrup
    7. 1/2 cup chopped pecans

- Instructions:

    1. Preheat oven to 325°F (160°C) and line a baking sheet with parchment paper.
    2. In a bowl, whisk together flour, cornstarch, and salt.
    3. Cream butter and powdered sugar, then mix in maple syrup.
    4. Gradually add dry ingredients and fold in pecans.
    5. Roll dough into a log and slice into rounds.
    6. Bake for 12-15 minutes until golden.

Lemon Meringue Bars

- Ingredients:

    1. 1 1/2 cups all-purpose flour
    2. 1/4 cup sugar
    3. 1/2 cup unsalted butter
    4. 1/4 tsp salt
    5. 1 cup sugar (for filling)
    6. 3 large eggs (for filling)
    7. 1/2 cup lemon juice
    8. 1/4 tsp salt (for filling)
    9. 1/4 tsp baking powder (for meringue)
    10. 3 large egg whites (for meringue)
    11. 1/4 cup sugar (for meringue)

- Instructions:

    1. Preheat oven to 350°F (175°C).
    2. Mix flour, sugar, butter, and salt, then press into the bottom of a baking pan.
    3. Bake for 15-20 minutes.
    4. For the filling, whisk eggs, sugar, lemon juice, and salt, then pour over the crust.

5. Bake for 15-20 minutes.

6. For the meringue, beat egg whites and sugar until stiff peaks form.

7. Spread meringue on top and bake for 10 minutes.

Chocolate Covered Pretzels

- Ingredients:

    1. Pretzels (mini or rods)

    2. 1 cup semisweet chocolate chips

    3. 1 tbsp coconut oil (optional for smoothness)

- Instructions:

    1. Melt chocolate and coconut oil together in a microwave or double boiler.

    2. Dip pretzels into chocolate, then place on parchment paper to set.

    3. Let cool for 1 hour.

Poppy Seed Lemon Cake

- Ingredients:

    1. 1 1/2 cups all-purpose flour
    2. 1 1/2 tsp baking powder
    3. 1/4 tsp salt
    4. 1/2 cup unsalted butter, softened
    5. 1 cup sugar
    6. 3 large eggs
    7. 1/4 cup lemon juice
    8. 1 tbsp lemon zest
    9. 1 tbsp poppy seeds

- Instructions:

    1. Preheat oven to 350°F (175°C) and grease a loaf pan.
    2. Mix flour, baking powder, and salt.
    3. Cream butter and sugar, then add eggs one at a time.
    4. Stir in lemon juice, zest, poppy seeds, and dry ingredients.
    5. Pour into the pan and bake for 40-45 minutes.

Toffee Almond Cookies

- Ingredients:

    1. 1 1/2 cups all-purpose flour
    2. 1/2 tsp baking soda
    3. 1/4 tsp salt
    4. 1 cup unsalted butter, softened
    5. 3/4 cup brown sugar, packed
    6. 1 large egg
    7. 1 tsp vanilla extract
    8. 1/2 cup toffee bits
    9. 1/2 cup chopped almonds

- Instructions:

    1. Preheat oven to 350°F (175°C).
    2. In a bowl, mix flour, baking soda, and salt.
    3. In another bowl, cream butter and brown sugar. Add egg and vanilla.
    4. Gradually add the dry ingredients, then fold in toffee bits and almonds.
    5. Scoop dough onto a baking sheet and bake for 10-12 minutes.